SHATTERED TO PIECES

Grief and God's Restoration

ATOSHA LOGAN

Copyright © 2020 by Atosha Logan

All rights reserved. No part of this book may be reproduced or used in any manner without the written permission of the copyright owner, except for the use of quotations in a book review.

For more information, address Atosha Logan, Author:
herlegacy@alegacytolivefor.com
www.alegacytolivefor.com

The events and conversations in this book have been set down to the best of the author's ability, although some names and/or details have been changed to protect the privacy of individuals.

Book Design by Atosha Logan

ISBN 978-1-7362267-0-4 (paperback)
ISBN 978-1-7362267-1-1 (Ebook)

This paperback edition was first published in 2020

Atosha Logan, Author & Publisher
herlegacy@alegacytolivefor.com
www.alegacytolivefor.com

Table of Contents

The Author 2

In Loving Memory, Mom 4

Introduction 6

Shattered Piece #1 Excuse me, What Did You Just Say? 8

Shattered Piece #2 We are in this together! 16

Shattered Piece #3 When the going gets tough, the tough gets going! 24

Shattered Piece #4 Who has your back? 33

Shattered Piece #5 Peace that surpasses all understanding 42

Shattered Piece #6 When you took your last breath! 51

Shattered Piece #7 Memories of yesterday 61

Shattered Piece #8 Living the Legacy you left behind! 71

Shattered Piece #9 The "Firsts" without you! 82

Shattered Piece #10 There is Purpose Behind this Pain 91

Putting the Pieces Back Together 100

Strategies for Self-care while grieving 104

What I need from others (support system) 107

Stages of Grief 109

Memory Box 111

Goodbye Letter 114

Acknowledgements 116

Shattered To Pieces.

Copyright © 2020 by Atosha Logan

The Author

Mrs. Atosha Logan

Atosha Logan is the author and publisher of the book, **Shattered To Pieces**. She is a proud daughter, wife, and mother of three children. She values time with God and her family more than anything.

She obtained her Bachelor's degree from the University of Florida, a Master's degree, and a Specialist Degree from Nova Southeastern University.

As an education leader, she understands the importance of meeting people where they are and helping them get where they need to be. She uses her life's experiences to testify that, with God, you can get through whatever obstacle lies ahead.

Atosha is a strong woman of the Christian faith and believes in the Word of God. Without the support of her family, close friends, and God, she doesn't know how she would have survived the passing of her beloved mother and best friend, Willie Mae. The heartache, grief, trials, and tribulations associated with the death of her mother were the driving forces behind writing the book, **Shattered To Pieces**.

Shattered To Pieces.

Copyright © 2020 by Atosha Logan

In Loving Memory, Mom

Willie Mae
1951-2019

Shattered To Pieces is dedicated to my mother, Willie Mae! She was my absolute best friend and the best mother in the world. She was the epitome of class, grace, style, poise, love, and leadership. She never met a stranger. I am who I am today because of my mother. I couldn't have imagined life without her.

When you passed in my arms, EVERYTHING around me Shattered To Pieces!

Nothing can separate the love between a mother and a daughter.

Mom, you will always be in my heart!

Love always to the moon and back,
Atosha Logan

INTRODUCTION
SHATTERED TO PIECES

Copyright © 2020 by Atosha Logan

Introduction

Grief is an emotional response to a significant loss. It weighs heavily on your heart, and you can experience great sorrow or regret. It can be a physical, a social, or an occupational loss.

This book is intended to provide an opportunity to go through the grieving process while reading, reflecting, journaling, and applying Biblical scripture.

You are not alone; others have been in the very space that you are in now. It doesn't matter what your job title is, your educational background, or your marital status. The pain experienced through grief hurts like no other. Grief is a natural reaction to loss. God promises that He will never leave us nor forsake us, and we must understand that He is restoring us in the shattered areas of our lives.

Shattered To Pieces.

SHATTERED PIECE #1

EXCUSE ME,
WHAT DID YOU JUST SAY?

Copyright © 2020 by Atosha Logan

Shattered Piece #1

Excuse me, What Did You Just Say?

I remember the call as if it were yesterday. My husband and I were sleeping, and the phone rang in the middle of the night. I answered, and on the other end of the phone line was a voice I've heard over a million times. That familiar voice was my dear mother's. As soon as I said, "hello", she began to speak with great despair that she had something to tell me. I couldn't begin to fathom what this news could possibly be; we talk about everything. I know all her business as she knows mine. She was literally my best friend —what news could she have that I didn't already know? She took a deep breath as she uttered the words, "I have really bad news. I have cancer, and it is stage 3."

Hearing the news, my heart stopped, and I was speechless. A thousand questions ran through my mind. Cancer? What type? How long have you known? What were your symptoms? Wait a minute, when were you sick? In that very moment, the only words that could come out of my mouth were "Excuse me, what did you just say?" Hoping it all was just a dream.

My *world* SHATTERED TO PIECES!

Shattered To Pieces.

A Safe Space to Reflect

> **What news have you received that took your breath away and left you speechless?**
>
> **If you had the opportunity to respond differently, what would you do and why?**
>
> **What questions do you have for God?**

Use this space to respond to the Shattered To Pieces chapter question(s). Be sure to include your feelings.

Copyright © 2020 by Atosha Logan

Shattered To Pieces.

The Word of God says...

Psalms 23:4

What is God saying to you in this scripture?

What words stood out?

How can I apply these Biblical truths to my life or situation?

Pray through the scripture and ask God to change your heart. Thank Him and ask for wisdom, strength, and courage to understand how to apply these truths to your situation.

The Word of God says...

Psalms 31:1

What is God saying to you in this scripture?

What words stood out?

How can I apply these Biblical truths to my life or situation?

Pray through the scripture and ask God to change your heart. Thank Him and ask for wisdom, strength, and courage to understand how to apply these truths to your situation.

Emotional Check Up

In this moment, how do you feel about your situation?

Right now, what do I need for myself? From others?

Copyright © 2020 by Atosha Logan

Let's Say a Prayer

Lord, I come before you with Thanksgiving, even amid bad news. I am at a loss for words. Your Word promises to hear our prayers. No matter what it looks like, Lord, I trust your will and I trust your way. Lord God, you are the Alpha and the Omega, and you know the beginning from the end. I thank you, Lord God, that I will be stronger in my walk with you. Even when I lack understanding, you are with me through any trial and tribulation I may go through, and I am very thankful that you are there with me.

Shattered To Pieces.

Shattered Piece #2

We are in this together!

Now that I have had time to collect my thoughts and emotions, where do we go from here? My mother has cancer. Cancer doesn't mean a death sentence. Others have survived. You can beat this.

What are our next steps? What are your treatment options? When is the next appointment? How are you feeling? Why didn't you tell me right away? Did you tell anyone else?

What do you need from me? I have so many questions and I don't know where to start. All I know is that without a shadow of a doubt, we are in this together!

My mother served multiple roles in my life. She was a mother, best friend, and sister to me. She knew how to play each role well. She had my back in every area of my life.

When she was hurt, I was hurt. When she cried, I cried. When she was in pain, I was in pain as well. She was one of my biggest supporters. Now, she needed me to support her. Mom, you will not have to fight this battle alone.

A Safe Space to Reflect

> In what ways have the troubles of life deepened your dependence on God?
>
> How do you need Jesus to hold things together for you right now?
>
> Do you believe that through the trials and triumphs of your life, he is your support system?

Use this space to respond to the Shattered To Pieces chapter question(s). Be sure to include your feelings

Copyright © 2020 by Atosha Logan

The Word of God says...
1 Thessalonians 5:11

What is God saying to you in this scripture?

What words stood out?

How can I apply these Biblical truths to my life or situation?

Pray through the scripture and ask God to change your heart. Thank Him and ask for wisdom, strength, and courage to understand how to apply these truths to your situation.

Shattered To Pieces.

The Word of God says...
Psalms 121:1-8

What is God saying to you in this scripture?

What words stood out?

How can I apply these Biblical truths to my life or situation?

Pray through the scripture and ask God to change your heart. Thank Him and ask for wisdom, strength, and courage to understand how to apply these truths to your situation.

Copyright © 2020 by Atosha Logan

The Word of God says...
Psalms 3:5

What is God saying to you in this scripture?

What words stood out?

How can I apply these Biblical truths to my life or situation?

Pray through the scripture and ask God to change your heart. Thank Him and ask for wisdom, strength, and courage to understand how to apply these truths to your situation.

Emotional Check Up

In this moment, how do you feel about your situation?

Right now, what do I need for myself? From others?

Copyright © 2020 by Atosha Logan

Let's Say a Prayer

Lord, I praise you for being the ultimate support system. I thank you, Lord God, that you continue to wrap your loving arms around me and comfort me in a time of need. I thank you, Lord, for having a listening ear to hear my troubles, and you know my heart. I need to intercede for someone else. Give me the strength to endure and support my loved one during this trying time. I thank you, Lord God, for your continued protection, guidance, and provision. No matter what I go through, Lord God, when I need you, you are always there for me.

Shattered Piece #3

When the going gets tough, the tough gets going!

My mom was determined to fight, and I fought with her. We listened to the doctors' reports, and the prognosis seemed manageable, but whew, this is tough. All the doctors' appointments, the medication you must take, and the assistive equipment needed are a lot to juggle alone. Treatment was complex and intense, but my mom refused to quit, and she continued to push through no matter what it felt like or looked like. My mom was one tough cookie, and I aspired to be at least half the woman she was.

My mother's fight was so strong that others didn't have a clue about her diagnosis or the seriousness of her illness. My mother was a prideful woman who kept her personal life just that; personal. She decided to keep her situation a secret from many. I honored her wishes and kept many of the details of her diagnosis under lock and key. She wanted people to keep loving her just because they did. She didn't want her authentic relationships to change because of her diagnosis or prognosis. She continued to keep her faith in God and kept a smile on her face through it all. Her strength is what gave me strength.

My world Shattered To Pieces.

A Safe Space to Reflect

> **Do you really believe the Lord can use your situation to bring glory to himself?**
> **What keeps your trust in the Lord during this time?**
> **How can your situation create something new in your life or be used to bless others?**
> **How can God cause a difficult circumstance to "work together for good" in your life?**

Use this space to respond to the Shattered To Pieces chapter question(s). Be sure to include your feelings.

Copyright © 2020 by Atosha Logan

The Word of God says...
Philippians 4:4-6

What is God saying to you in this scripture?

What words stood out?

How can I apply these Biblical truths to my life or situation?

Pray through the scripture and ask God to change your heart. Thank Him and ask for wisdom, strength, and courage to understand how to apply these truths to your situation.

Shattered To Pieces.

The Word of God says...
Joshua 1:7-9

What is God saying to you in this scripture?

What words stood out?

How can I apply these Biblical truths to my life or situation?

Pray through the scripture and ask God to change your heart. Thank Him and ask for wisdom, strength, and courage to understand how to apply these truths to your situation.

Copyright © 2020 by Atosha Logan

The Word of God says...
Psalms 56:3-4

What is God saying to you in this scripture?

What words stood out?

How can I apply these Biblical truths to my life or situation?

Pray through the scripture and ask God to change your heart. Thank Him and ask for wisdom, strength, and courage to understand how to apply these truths to your situation.

Emotional Check Up

In this moment, how do you feel about your situation?

Right now, what do I need for myself? From others?

Copyright © 2020 by Atosha Logan

Shattered To Pieces.

Let's Say a Prayer

Lord, thank you for your greatness. Thank you that when I am weak, you are strong. Lord, remove any distractions that keep me from spending time with you. Don't let the enemy win! Please give me a measure of your strength so that I might not give in to discouragement, deception, fear, unbelief, and doubt! Help me honor you in all my ways.

Copyright © 2020 by Atosha Logan

SHATTERED PIECE #4
WHO HAS YOUR BACK?

Shattered Piece #4

Who has your back?

The strength of a support system is vitally important to your healing.

I attended every doctor's appointment in person or on the phone. She started treatment, and the strong, independent mother I have known needed support. As one of the side effects of chemo, my mother's hair fell out in clumps. To display my love and support, I made a private in-home appointment with our barber. She made the big chop and shaved the rest of her hair. To her surprise, I cut all my long hair off just like hers. After all, we are in this together.

Who has your back? Who's there for you in your time of need? Often, we help so many people and we don't get the same in return. When you are at your lowest, your dear and trusted family and friends should be there to support you through your tough times. While I was the support system for my mother, my close family and friends were my support system. It hurt that I couldn't change or control the situation. All I ever wanted was for her to feel better and be healed. I needed people who could intercede and pray for me through this. I have learned that during the process, it is essential that even when you don't have all the details of the situation, if a family or friend needs you to have their back, you should do so.

My world Shattered To Pieces!

Copyright © 2020 by Atosha Logan

Shattered To Pieces.

A Safe Space to Reflect

> **How does helping another person change us?**
>
> **How do you find a way to support other people who cope with their circumstances differently than the way you would?**
>
> **What do you believe Jesus is asking you to do today in your situation?**

Use this space to respond to the Shattered To Pieces chapter question(s). Be sure to include your feelings.

Copyright © 2020 by Atosha Logan

The Word of God says...
John 15:12

What is God saying to you in this scripture?

What words stood out?

How can I apply these Biblical truths to my life or situation?

Pray through the scripture and ask God to change your heart. Thank Him and ask for wisdom, strength, and courage to understand how to apply these truths to your situation.

Shattered To Pieces.

The Word of God says...
Galatians 6:2

What is God saying to you in this scripture?

What words stood out?

How can I apply these Biblical truths to my life or situation?

Pray through the scripture and ask God to change your heart. Thank Him and ask for wisdom, strength, and courage to understand how to apply these truths to your situation.

Copyright © 2020 by Atosha Logan

The Word of God says...
Romans 12:13

What is God saying to you in this scripture?

What words stood out?

How can I apply these Biblical truths to my life or situation?

Pray through the scripture and ask God to change your heart. Thank Him and ask for wisdom, strength, and courage to understand how to apply these truths to your situation.

Emotional Check Up

In this moment, how do you feel about your situation?

Right now, what do I need for myself? From others?

Copyright © 2020 by Atosha Logan

Let's Say a Prayer

Lord, sometimes it feels like you have left me in the battle. We know that you are with us, but sometimes our feelings of aloneness, fear, and anxiety take over. The Enemy desires to sift me as wheat. My cries to you seem to go unanswered. Oh, how I long to hear that still small voice. I know you are at work, but help me trust you even when I ask questions.

Shattered Piece #5

Peace that surpasses all understanding

My mother fought with tooth and nail. She followed the doctors' exact orders. She changed her diet. She went through treatment, and she took all the medicine prescribed, but suddenly her health took a turn for the worse. She was on life support, and all I could do was beg the Lord for a miracle. If I could only hear her voice one more time, it would be a constant reminder of how much I loved her and how much she loved me. God granted that miracle. The joy I felt when my mother opened her eyes, breathed on her own, and asked me, "What's going on?" was the best day of my life. All in all, no matter what, my mother continued to fight as she pushed through the obstacles and the pain. Her body was very weak, but her spiritual strength was remarkable.

She needed my support more than anything now. She needed me to care for her around the clock. I immediately readjusted my entire life to meet her medical needs. I know that if the shoe were on the other foot, my mother would have done the very same thing.

We were later hit with the unbearable news, the news that my mother knew in her heart, but she allowed the doctor to tell me. It was time for me to say to the person that I loved with every fiber in my body that there was nothing else that could be done medically. It was time for comfort and to make the best of a challenging situation. In that very moment, my mother looked at me and said, "All is well". She said, "I lived my life. I traveled everywhere I wanted to go. I bought what I wanted. I was able to see you grow as a mature adult. I spent time with my grandchildren, and I have lived the life that God desired of me. Though I wish I could stay a little longer, I am at peace with God's decision." We embraced each other as the tears flowed like a river.

Even in the midst of her situation, my mother was still worried about me. She called key people in my life to tell them that I will need them now more than anything.

My World Shattered To Pieces

A Safe Space to Reflect

> **What are the challenges that come when you let go to let God have his way?**
>
> **How do you need Jesus to hold things together for you right now?**
>
> **What ideas or images come to mind when you hear the phrase "God's will"?**

Use this space to respond to the Shattered To Pieces chapter question(s). Be sure to include your feelings.

Shattered To Pieces.

The Word of God says...
Proverbs 3:1-6

What is God saying to you in this scripture?

What words stood out?

How can I apply these Biblical truths to my life or situation?

Pray through the scripture and ask God to change your heart. Thank Him and ask for wisdom, strength, and courage to understand how to apply these truths to your situation.

Shattered To Pieces.

The Word of God says...
Psalms 16:7-11

What is God saying to you in this scripture?

What words stood out?

How can I apply these Biblical truths to my life or situation?

Pray through the scripture and ask God to change your heart. Thank Him and ask for wisdom, strength, and courage to understand how to apply these truths to your situation.

Emotional Check Up

In this moment, how do you feel about your situation?

Right now, what do I need for myself? From others?

Let's Say a Prayer

Lord, help me not to lean on my own understanding, but to acknowledge You in everything, so that You can direct my words, thoughts, and actions. Father God, my heart is filled with chaos, heartbreak, and confusion. I feel as if I am drowning in my circumstances, and my heart is filled with fear and confusion. I really need the strength and peace that only You can give. Right now, I choose to trust in You because You are the one who knows what I need to get through this situation.

Copyright © 2020 by Atosha Logan

SHATTERED PIECE #6

WHEN YOU TOOK YOUR LAST BREATH!

Shattered Piece #6

When you took your last breath!

That dreaded day was near, and it was time for God's purpose, will, and plan to come to fruition. What else can I do? Is it too late to ask God again for a miracle? Am I being selfish by keeping you here? By wanting you to stay, do I continue to watch you suffer? No matter how I felt, God continued to give me clarity that he needed her more than I did.

We spent many late nights talking as a mother and daughter should. We watched your favorite shows and recorded all our conversations to use as memories to come. You gave me all your wishes for your funeral arrangements, and you told me what to do with your personal items. We had all of life's most challenging conversations. You repeatedly reminded me that you will always be in my heart! You spent time or had conversations with your closest friends and family. My goal was to make your last days the best they could be before you drifted into a deep sleep. Your body began to get cold, and each breath began to get further and further apart. The dreaded reality that you were transitioning was closer and closer.

As your blood pressure and oxygen levels dropped, the unthinkable was near, but you opened your eyes one last time. I believe you asked God for permission to talk to me one last time. You gazed into my eyes for reassurance that I would be OK. I gave you my blessing. I told you repeatedly, "I loved you and I wouldn't be who I am if it weren't for you." In that moment, you looked to the heavens as you took your last breath.

My World Shattered To Pieces

A Safe Space to Reflect

Identify what you consider to be the most significant loss or shattering experience you've ever had?

What did you learn about God through that experience?

How can this experience be overcome through prayer?

Use this space to respond to the Shattered To Pieces chapter question(s). Be sure to include your feelings.

The Word of God says...
Psalms 34:18

What is God saying to you in this scripture?

What words stood out?

How can I apply these Biblical truths to my life or situation?

Pray through the scripture and ask God to change your heart. Thank Him and ask for wisdom, strength, and courage to understand how to apply these truths to your situation.

Shattered To Pieces.

The Word of God says...
Psalms 147:3

What is God saying to you in this scripture?

What words stood out?

How can I apply these Biblical truths to my life or situation?

Pray through the scripture and ask God to change your heart. Thank Him and ask for wisdom, strength, and courage to understand how to apply these truths to your situation.

Copyright © 2020 by Atosha Logan

The Word of God says...
Matthew 5:4

What is God saying to you in this scripture?

What words stood out?

How can I apply these Biblical truths to my life or situation?

Pray through the scripture and ask God to change your heart. Thank Him and ask for wisdom, strength, and courage to understand how to apply these truths to your situation.

Shattered To Pieces.

The Word of God says...
Revelation 21:4

What is God saying to you in this scripture?

What words stood out?

How can I apply these Biblical truths to my life or situation?

Pray through the scripture and ask God to change your heart. Thank Him and ask for wisdom, strength, and courage to understand how to apply these truths to your situation.

Emotional Check Up

In this moment, how do you feel about your situation?

Right now, what do I need for myself? From others?

Let's Say a Prayer

Lord, my heart is broken, but You are near. My spirit is crushed, but You are my rescuer. Your Word is my hope and strength. It revives me and comforts me, especially now. Lord, I recognize my need for a Savior because I can't get through this on my own. My soul and spirit feel weak, but you are the breath of life within me. You are my help, the one who sustains me. I am weak, but you are strong. You bless those who mourn, and I trust You to bless my family and me with all we need. You will rescue me from this dark cloud of despair because You will get the glory in this.

Copyright © 2020 by Atosha Logan

Shattered Piece #7

Memories of yesterday

I can't believe you are gone. I keep replaying yesterday over and over. This must be a bad dream. Where is my best friend? Where is my mother? Why couldn't she stay a little longer? The pain and the memories of yesterday will forever stick in my mind and in my heart. How do I go on? Am I fulfilling all your wishes? These were all the questions that ran through my mind as I continued to reflect on yesterday. You are gone to be with the Lord, and what am I supposed to do without you? How is this my new normal? We talked 100 times a day, and now I will never hear your voice again.

I have given condolences to so many people before, but never in a million years did I understand the pain of losing a mother. No one will ever be able to love me like she did. There could never be a replacement. My mother was my favorite girl, and only God can get me through this. I thank God for the time and love I shared with my beloved mother. She was like no other.

The pain, the memories, and the hurt of yesterday will never go away!

My World Shattered To Pieces

A Safe Space to Reflect

> How did experiencing the loss of a loved one change the way you see other people?
>
> How did it change the way you treat other people who are going through a similar loss?
>
> How do you typically respond to painful situations?

Use this space to respond to the Shattered To Pieces chapter question(s). Be sure to include your feelings.

Shattered To Pieces.

The Word of God says...
Philippians 4:7

What is God saying to you in this scripture?

What words stood out?

How can I apply these Biblical truths to my life or situation?

Pray through the scripture and ask God to change your heart. Thank Him and ask for wisdom, strength, and courage to understand how to apply these truths to your situation.

Copyright © 2020 by Atosha Logan

The Word of God says...
Genesis 31:49

What is God saying to you in this scripture?

What words stood out?

How can I apply these Biblical truths to my life or situation?

Pray through the scripture and ask God to change your heart. Thank Him and ask for wisdom, strength, and courage to understand how to apply these truths to your situation.

Shattered To Pieces.

The Word of God says...
Ecclesiastes 3:1-4

What is God saying to you in this scripture?

What words stood out?

How can I apply these Biblical truths to my life or situation?

Pray through the scripture and ask God to change your heart. Thank Him and ask for wisdom, strength, and courage to understand how to apply these truths to your situation.

Copyright © 2020 by Atosha Logan

The Word of God says...
Lamentations 3:32

What is God saying to you in this scripture?

What words stood out?

How can I apply these Biblical truths to my life or situation?

Pray through the scripture and ask God to change your heart. Thank Him and ask for wisdom, strength, and courage to understand how to apply these truths to your situation.

Emotional Check Up

In this moment, how do you feel about your situation?

Right now, what do I need for myself? From others?

Copyright © 2020 by Atosha Logan

Let's Say a Prayer

God, you never said it was going to be easy. You said, "Trust me." My faith is strong, and I give myself to You. I will live this life with gratitude. Appreciating every little thing and moment, its difficulties and pleasures. For all this and more, I am grateful.

You are the Alpha and Omega and the beginning and the end. This didn't catch you by surprise. I need you and your strength, oh Lord. Comfort me during this time.

Copyright © 2020 by Atosha Logan

SHATTERED PIECE #8

LIVING THE LEGACY
YOU LEFT BEHIND

Shattered Piece #8

Living the Legacy you left behind!

My mother was the epitome of poise, class, intellect, love, and leadership. She taught me everything I know. A Legacy is when someone leaves something behind of value. She taught me how to carry myself as a young woman and understand my worth.

She was my role model. She is the reason why I am who I am today. It was her goal to instill as much as she could in me so that I was more successful than she was. She loved to sit proud and say, "That is my daughter." She taught me how to cook, budget money, run a household, stay educated, manage a career, care for my children, reverence God and cherish time with close family and friends. She was my hero. Her greatest desire was to see me accomplish all of my dreams and I am glad she was able to be right by my side through most of them.

She also taught me at an early age that a woman is seen and not heard. Not that women should be quiet but rather everyone should recognize your value when you enter the room without you telling them who you are. No one explains what a $100 bill is, you can simply see it and know it's worth. She was a true model of this practice.

She was educated, articulate, talented, and beautiful inside and out. She lived her life to the fullest. She did what she wanted to do, went where she wanted to go, bought what she wanted to buy and said what she wanted to say.

My mother had a gift to minister and help others; whether it was to cook a meal, visit in your time of need, serve as a mentor or pray for you. She never met a stranger. She walked in love towards people everywhere she went. Words cannot describe the love my mother and I shared.

One of my mother's last words to me was, "Tosha I prepared you to be successful in everything in life except how to live without me." She was right. I don't know where to begin. No one will be able to fill that void, but her legacy shall continue in me.

My World Shattered To Pieces

A Safe Space to Reflect

> **What do you believe you are responsible for teaching and/or leaving for the next generation?**
>
> **When have you most strongly felt that you were living the kind of life that God created you to live?**
>
> **What does it look like to let your light shine before men?**

Use this space to respond to the Shattered To Pieces chapter question(s). Be sure to include your feelings.

The Word of God says...
Proverbs 22:6

What is God saying to you in this scripture?

What words stood out?

How can I apply these Biblical truths to my life or situation?

Pray through the scripture and ask God to change your heart. Thank Him and ask for wisdom, strength, and courage to understand how to apply these truths to your situation.

Shattered To Pieces.

The Word of God says...
Jeremiah 29:11

What is God saying to you in this scripture?

What words stood out?

How can I apply these Biblical truths to my life or situation?

Pray through the scripture and ask God to change your heart. Thank Him and ask for wisdom, strength, and courage to understand how to apply these truths to your situation.

The Word of God says...
Philippians 3:13

What is God saying to you in this scripture?

What words stood out?

How can I apply these Biblical truths to my life or situation?

Pray through the scripture and ask God to change your heart. Thank Him and ask for wisdom, strength, and courage to understand how to apply these truths to your situation.

Shattered To Pieces.

The Word of God says...
Hebrews 10:35-36

What is God saying to you in this scripture?

What words stood out?

How can I apply these Biblical truths to my life or situation?

Pray through the scripture and ask God to change your heart. Thank Him and ask for wisdom, strength, and courage to understand how to apply these truths to your situation.

Emotional Check Up

In this moment, how do you feel about your situation?

Right now, what do I need for myself? From others?

Shattered To Pieces.

Copyright © 2020 by Atosha Logan

Let's Say a Prayer

Lord, forgive me for the times I choose to follow my own will rather than Yours. I know Your plan for my life is the highest and has my best interest in mind. I was created in response to Your will before You formed me in my mother's womb. Thank you for the purpose in my life. God, you purposefully created me to be a light in darkness. Thank you for making our family with the purpose. I strive to fill that purpose daily.
Today I choose to seek You and obey Your Word.

Shattered To Pieces.

SHATTERED PIECE #9
THE "FIRSTS" WITHOUT YOU!

Shattered Piece #9

The "Firsts" without you!

Adjusting without you was hard, but experiencing the "firsts" without you was even harder. You might ask what the "firsts" are? The first are the significant events and holidays you are experiencing without your loved one for the first time. The first holiday, Mother's Day, was the hardest. It was a month after you died. How do I celebrate a day designed to show love to the very person who isn't here? It was hard even to celebrate being a mother myself. Your birthday, holidays, my birthday, and my children's birthdays without my mother were hard. Thanksgiving and Christmas just aren't the same. I miss you the most during these times. I've never spent a holiday without you. These are the days when you would typically be right by our side to celebrate and fellowship. We desperately miss your presence, and I can't count how many times I have tried to pick up the phone to share these precious moments with you.

Shattered To Pieces.

A Safe Space to Reflect

> **How is your life been changed by meaningful encounters with God during this process?**
>
> **What have you learned about your family during this time?**
>
> **What blessings have come out of this difficult situation?**

Use this space to respond to the Shattered To Pieces chapter question(s). Be sure to include your feelings.

Copyright © 2020 by Atosha Logan

**The Word of God says...
Romans 15:13**

What is God saying to you in this scripture?

What words stood out?

How can I apply these Biblical truths to my life or situation?

Pray through the scripture and ask God to change your heart. Thank Him and ask for wisdom, strength, and courage to understand how to apply these truths to your situation.

Shattered To Pieces.

The Word of God says...
Luke 1:78-79

What is God saying to you in this scripture?

What words stood out?

How can I apply these Biblical truths to my life or situation?

Pray through the scripture and ask God to change your heart. Thank Him and ask for wisdom, strength, and courage to understand how to apply these truths to your situation.

Copyright © 2020 by Atosha Logan

The Word of God says...
Psalms 30:5

What is God saying to you in this scripture?

What words stood out?

How can I apply these Biblical truths to my life or situation?

Pray through the scripture and ask God to change your heart. Thank Him and ask for wisdom, strength, and courage to understand how to apply these truths to your situation.

Shattered To Pieces.

The Word of God says...
Romans 8:18

What is God saying to you in this scripture?

What words stood out?

How can I apply these Biblical truths to my life or situation?

Pray through the scripture and ask God to change your heart. Thank Him and ask for wisdom, strength, and courage to understand how to apply these truths to your situation.

Emotional Check Up

In this moment, how do you feel about your situation?

Right now, what do I need for myself? From others?

Let's Say a Prayer

Lord, I'm here today with open arms and an open heart. I am ready to depend on you to help me through this and all it will bring my way. Lord, heal my heart and hurt with peace. Fill my void with joy, knowing that my loved one is resting in your arms in Heaven. Please help me with guidance, strength, provision, and protection. As I face tough and challenging situations, help me remember that I am Your child. Help me live today in a way that brings honor and glory to Your holy name.

Copyright © 2020 by Atosha Logan

SHATTERED PIECE #10

THERE IS PURPOSE
BEHIND THIS PAIN

Shattered Piece #10

There is a Purpose Behind this Pain

Throughout this journey of grief, I have learned a lot as I continue to seek God's will for my life. My mom's life and death remind me every day of my purpose. She touched the lives of so many people.

My mother instilled a legacy within me. It is my responsibility to ensure that the legacy continues. Even though my mother isn't here physically her spirit is always near and dear in my heart.

The various situations that we go through aren't for us but for us to help others through. Since the passing of my mother I have encountered so many other individuals that share the same type of relationship with their mothers as I had. The hardest part of grief is thinking you are alone. Thinking that others don't quite understand your level of pain and hurt. I want to use the pain in my heart to share with the world that you are not alone. There are others going through the very same thing that you are. It is important to share some of the strategies that I used to help cope during grief and let it be a blessing to someone else.

My World Shattered To Pieces

Copyright © 2020 by Atosha Logan

A Safe Space to Reflect

> **What feelings or emotions do you experience when you think about fulfilling your purpose?**
>
> **What spiritual gifts have you been given that can be used to bless someone else?**
>
> **How will you intentionally use your experience to enhance God's Kingdom or your relationship with him?**

Use this space to respond to the Shattered To Pieces chapter question(s). Be sure to include your feelings.

Shattered To Pieces.

The Word of God says...
Psalms 35:22

What is God saying to you in this scripture?

What words stood out?

How can I apply these Biblical truths to my life or situation?

Pray through the scripture and ask God to change your heart. Thank Him and ask for wisdom, strength, and courage to understand how to apply these truths to your situation.

The Word of God says...
Psalms 119:28

What is God saying to you in this scripture?

What words stood out?

How can I apply these Biblical truths to my life or situation?

Pray through the scripture and ask God to change your heart. Thank Him and ask for wisdom, strength, and courage to understand how to apply these truths to your situation.

Shattered To Pieces.

The Word of God says...
John 14:27

What is God saying to you in this scripture?

What words stood out?

How can I apply these Biblical truths to my life or situation?

Pray through the scripture and ask God to change your heart. Thank Him and ask for wisdom, strength, and courage to understand how to apply these truths to your situation.

The Word of God says...
Romans 8:38-39

What is God saying to you in this scripture?

What words stood out?

How can I apply these Biblical truths to my life or situation?

Pray through the scripture and ask God to change your heart. Thank Him and ask for wisdom, strength, and courage to understand how to apply these truths to your situation.

Emotional Check Up

In this moment, how do you feel about your situation?

Right now, what do I need for myself? From others?

Copyright © 2020 by Atosha Logan

Let's Say a Prayer

Lord, thank you for using all things for your purposes. Thank you for having a perfect time and a perfect plan. Thank you for allowing everything into our lives to perfect, refine, renew, restore, heal, and complete our purpose. Lord, when I don't know when this "race" will end in my life. Please help me to stop trying to outrun my pain, but instead run the race before me with endurance. I know that because of you, I am ultimately a victor over all the trials and tribulations in my life. I know that nothing in this world can separate me from your everlasting love. Please give me the strength to continue to endure this trial. Thank you for your love for me that never ends!

Copyright © 2020 by Atosha Logan

Putting the Pieces Back Together

Dear (Deceased Name)	Our Best Memory...
I always wanted to say...	I love this the most about you...

Shattered To Pieces.

Putting the Pieces Back Together

Please forgive me for...	I really miss...
I will honor you by...	When you died, I...

Putting the Pieces Back Together

My worst memory is...	When I am alone, I...
You missed the following events...	I feel better when...

STRATEGIES OF SELFCARE

GRIEF CAN CAUSE YOUR HEALTH TO DETERIORATE. IT IS IMPORTANT THAT YOU TAKE CARE OF YOURSELF AS YOU GRIEVE.

Copyright © 2020 by Atosha Logan

Strategies for Self-care while grieving

★Cry when you want to

★ It's OK not to be OK

★Have a support system

★Seek therapy

★Journal your feelings

★Read a book

★Watch a movie

★Exercise

★Eat a healthy meal

★Listen to your favorite song

★Recite your favorite scripture/Pray

★Participate in activities you love

★Take deep breaths

★Join a grief group

★Talk to someone you trust

Shattered To Pieces.

Copyright © 2020 by Atosha Logan

WHAT I NEED FROM OTHERS

OFTEN TIMES, FAMILY AND FRIENDS DONT KNOW WHAT TO SAY OR DO DURING THIS TIME. SET BOUNDARIES AND EDUCATE LOVED ONES ON WHAT YOU NEED TO COPE WITH YOUR LOSS.

What I need from others (support system)

★Coping strategies
★Advice to cope
★Just be there
★Provide a listening ear
★Respect when I don't want to talk
★Invite me to enjoyable activities
★Patience
★Prayer
★Comforting Words
★ Frequent Check Ins (Spiritually, Physically, and Mentally)
★Ask if I want to hear stories about my loved one
★Don't take it personally if today isn't a good day
★Understand things that trigger emotions/mood swings
★Be sensitive about comments
★Allow me to offer the deceased's personal items before asking for them.
★The financial assets of the deceased will be shared with whom I desire.
★Don't put a timeframe on my grief

Shattered To Pieces.

Stages of Grief

There are five stages of grief, and they look different for everyone. You may not experience them all, or in order, but the stages you do go through will vary in intensity.

As you experience a stage, use the clouds to reflect on your emotions.

Denial
"This can't be happening!"

Anger
"Why is this happening to me?"

Bargaining
"I will do anything to change this!"

Depression
"What's the point of going on after this loss!"

Acceptance
"It's going to be OK!"

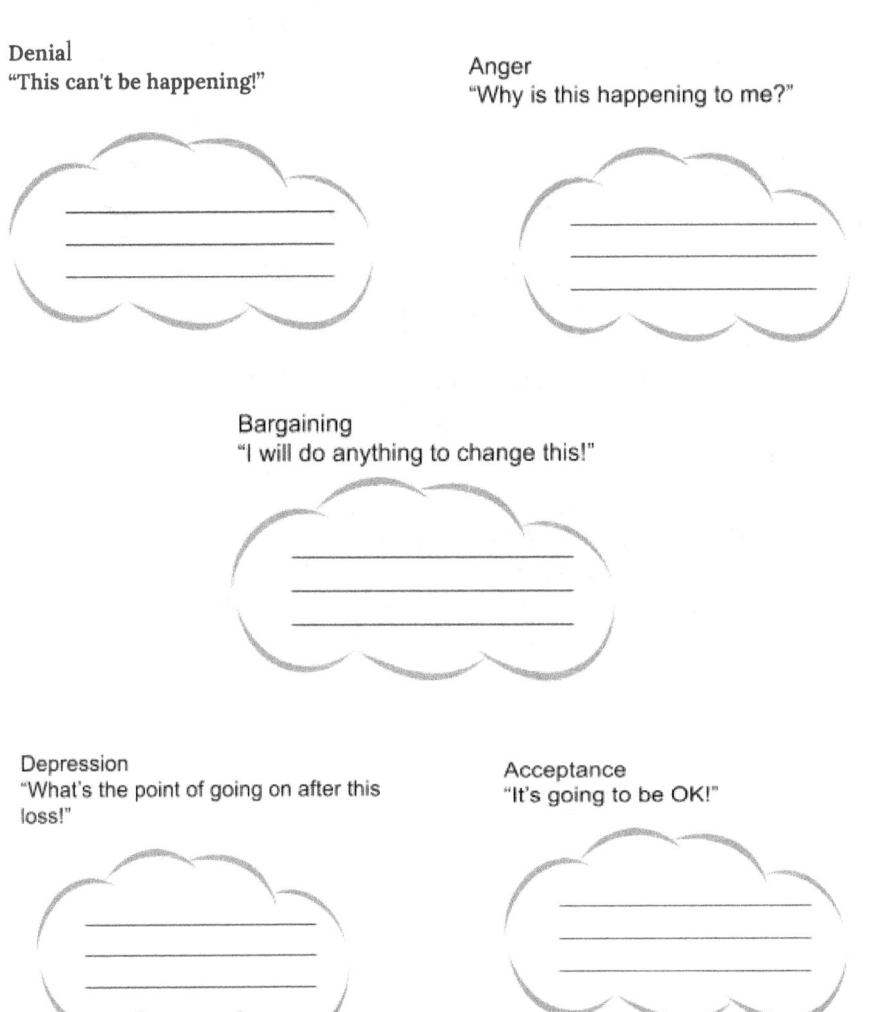

Copyright © 2020 by Atosha Logan

Shattered To Pieces.

Memory Box

Everything I never want to forget about...

Your LIFE

Your LEGACY

Your LOVE

THE GOODBYE LETTER

IF YOU WERE GRANTED ONE LAST OPPORTUNITY TO TALK TO YOUR LOVED ONE, WHAT WOULD YOU SAY? WRITE IT IN A LETTER.

Goodbye Letter

All the things I wish I could have said to you.

Dear_____

_____

_____

_____

_____

_____

_____

_____

_____

_____

_____

Shattered To Pieces.

Love,

Copyright © 2020 by Atosha Logan

Acknowledgements

Words can't express how much I appreciate the patience, love, and support shown by my wonderful husband, Shawn, and my three beautiful children: Jailan, James, and Jordin. My husband was there through all the late nights, wiping my tears and praying away my fears. My mom always referred to you as her "Favorite Son-In-Law," even though you were her ONLY son-in-law. Thank you for being the best husband in the world.

To my children, who were affectionately known as my mother's "GECKOS"! It amazes me how much you protect me as I grieve! I am honored to have such wonderful children who love me to the moon and back. It is my goal to be the best mother to each of you, as my mother was to me!

Writing this book was truly an emotional journey, as I had to relive painful memories. My family and "close" friends have been nothing less than my backbone during this process. God gave me the vision, and he supplied EVERYTHING I needed to make it happen. Obedience is better than sacrifice, and I am so glad I answered the call. God gets the GLORY in all of this!

www.ingramcontent.com/pod-product-compliance
Lightning Source LLC
Chambersburg PA
CBHW071859070526
44583CB00016B/1761